A whole street of cob at Drewsteignton, Devon.

Clay and Cob Buildings

John McC

A Shire book

Published in 2004 by Shire Publications Ltd,
Cromwell House, Church Street, Princes Risborough,
Buckinghamshire HP27 9AA, UK.
(Website: www.shirebooks.co.uk)

Copyright © 1983 and 2004 by John McCann.
First published 1983.
Second edition 1995.
Third edition, revised and illustrated in colour, 2004.
Shire Album 105. ISBN 0 7478 0579 2.
John McCann is hereby identified as the author of this
work in accordance with Section 77 of the Copyright,
Designs and Patents Act 1988.

British Library Cataloguing in Publication Data:
McCann, John
Clay and cob buildings. – 3rd ed. – (Shire album; 105)
1. Building, Clay – Great Britain – History
2. Cob (Building material)
3. Architecture, Domestic – Great Britain – History
I. Title
721'.04422'0941
ISBN 0 7478 0579 2.

Cover: *Cottages of chalk mud at Rockbourne, Hampshire. The top of the mud wall is tiled below the windows. The half-gable is of timber framing.*

ACKNOWLEDGEMENTS
I wish to express my gratitude to Martin Andrew, Dirk Bouwens, Elizabeth Bryan, Ray
Harrison, Kevin McCabe, Gerallt Nash, Gordon Pearson, Mathew Robinson, Greg
Stevenson, Elphin and Brenda Watkin, Eurwyn Wiliam, and members of the Devon Earth
Building Association, who have generously helped with information. Others were
acknowledged in the first and second editions; their contributions are incorporated in this,
the third edition, and they are remembered with gratitude. Those who have supplied
illustrations are acknowledged in the captions.
Except where stated otherwise in the captions, all the photographs are by the author.

Printed in Malta by Gutenberg Press Limited, Gudja Road,
Tarxien PLA 19, Malta.

Contents

Note on visiting

    Only three of the buildings illustrated in this book are open to the public – Marker's Cottage, Broadclyst, Devon, and Hardy's Cottage, Higher Bockhampton, Dorset, which belong to the National Trust, and the reconstructed *clom* cottage at the Museum of Welsh Life. All the others are privately owned. As internal surfaces are plastered there is rarely anything to see of the construction inside.

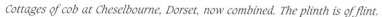

Cottages of cob at Cheselbourne, Dorset, now combined. The plinth is of flint.

A clay cottage at Buxhall, Suffolk, built by Copinger Hill. This is an early type, with the upper rooms partly in the roof; in 1843 Hill specified that the cottages should be of two full storeys. In 1839 this cottage was occupied by a wheelwright. An ancillary building of clay lump is shown to the left.

The four processes: cob, shuttered earth, clay lump and *pisé*

In many parts of Britain there are buildings and boundary walls made of unfired earth, which gives a distinctive character to the region. Houses of this construction are comfortable to live in, being warm in winter and cool in summer. They have been built of subsoil containing clay or chalk by one of four processes.

Cob

This method of building is usually associated with the West Country, but under other names it has been used in many parts of Britain. The word *cob* is first recorded in Cornwall in 1602. The form *clob* was used in Berkshire in the eighteenth century. In Wales the same material is called *clom* or *mwd*. In Buckinghamshire the local name is *witchert*. Elsewhere these buildings are usually described as *clay* or *mud*.

A clay cottage at Buxhall, Suffolk, of the type described by Copinger Hill in 1843. Originally Hill provided thatched roofs for the comfort of the tenants, but this has been replaced with asbestos tiles. Note the deep window reveals. The upper right-hand window is of cast iron; the others are modern replacements. The position of the original central doorway is just perceptible as a patch of different texture in the render.

Clay and Cob Buildings

John McCann

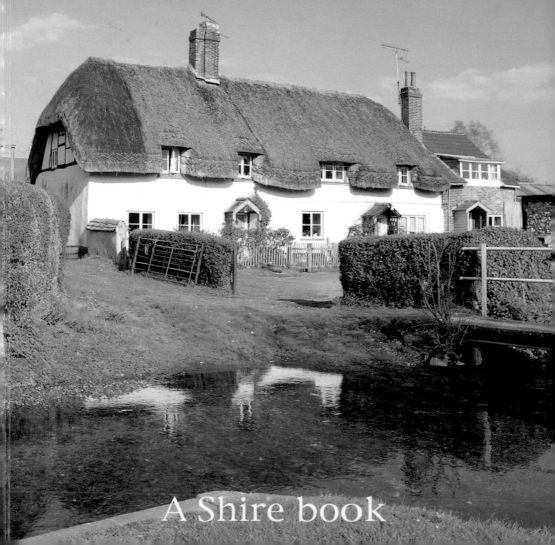

A Shire book

The commonest method of building with cob, which Dr R. W. Brunskill has called the 'slow process', was well described in Suffolk in 1843 by the Reverend Copinger Hill:

Clay for building should be a clay-marl. If the clay [soil] is not good, chalk and road-grit should be mixed with it... with moderate clay, say seven-tenths clay, two-tenths chalk, one tenth road-grit. The clay and chalk are raised and carted to a convenient spot of hard ground, where they are beaten to pieces by a heavy prong, and the stones picked out, and formed into a circular bed one foot thick and 20 feet in diameter [300 mm by 6 metres]. The bed is well watered, and trodden by horses... and while trodden, one man shakes short straw upon it with a fork, while another pulls it about with a prong, and throws the outside portions under the feet of the horses, and supplies a sufficiency of water. It can hardly be too much trodden... It is then rounded up and covered with straw until wanted for use... A pinning [foundation wall] of stonework 14 inches [350 mm] thick and one foot [300 mm] out of the ground is prepared. One man gets upon the pinning with a small three-pronged fork; his partner throws up to him small lumps of clay, the size of a double-fist, which he adroitly catches on the fork, and deposits on the wall, walking backwards. A height of 20 inches or 2 feet [500–600 mm] is built at one time; at intervals as the work proceeds the workmen coax the sides of the wall with spades and make it straight. It is then left to dry for a few days or longer; all depends on the weather. When dry another course is laid on until the requisite height is obtained. As the wall rises window-frames and door-frames are fixed; and when the roof is on the dauber cases [plasters] the walls inside and out with clay, corrects all defects and irregularities, and leaves it smooth and white. The clay for casing is prepared with more care than the body of the wall; old clay-wall worked up afresh makes the best casing.

Cob building was carried out in much the same way in other regions of Britain. Reports from some counties indicate that the

A boundary wall of chalk cob at Harwell, Oxfordshire. The 'raises', or courses, are clearly visible.

A thatched wall of chalk cob at Ashwell, Hertfordshire. Note the foundation wall of brickwork.

earth-straw mixture was trodden by cattle or donkeys; the *mud-mason* pressed each forkful into place with his boot; and the tool used to trim down the vertical surfaces could be a spade, a mattock, a hay knife or a *paring iron* (similar to a baker's peel but made of iron). What differed most between one place and another was the natural material available. Clay soils contain only a small proportion of pure clay, the remainder being made up of inert aggregates – silt, sand and gravel. In a few fortunate localities the subsoil could be used just as it came from the ground, but mostly it had to be *tempered*. Clay expands when it is wet and shrinks as it dries; to control the shrinkage evenly graded aggregates had to

An early-nineteenth-century 'slow process' clay cottage at Bambers Green, Takeley, Essex, close to Stansted Airport.

be added (the additives specified by Copinger Hill were appropriate for Buxhall in Suffolk, but they might be very different elsewhere). Judging the composition of the particular subsoil and knowing which aggregates to add in the appropriate quantities were traditional skills handed down by earlier generations of cob builders, derived from substantial experience with the local materials. Large quantities of straw were mixed in to assist handling, to provide fibrous reinforcement and to minimise and distribute the fine cracks formed as the material dried. Winter barley is said to produce the strongest straw for cob but in practice every kind of straw has been used – and where straw was not available many other kinds of natural fibre were substituted, such as hay, heather or broom.

Most cob walls were thicker than those described by Copinger Hill. Ancient farmhouses in Devon have walls 3 feet (900 mm) thick or more. By the eighteenth century it was common to build them 20–24 inches (500–600 mm) thick. Some cob walls reduce in thickness as they rise, with a step at first-floor level to support the floor joists. Usually they present a vertical surface outside even when the inner surface is *battered* (or inclined). The height of the *raises* or courses varies in different areas according to how high the local material would stand while wet without slumping. Even in the same building the raises may be of different heights – indicating that cob building was an irregular activity, perhaps carried out in the intervals between other jobs. Chimneys were of cob or stone, but the upper parts have now mostly been rebuilt in brickwork.

It was common practice to excavate the subsoil in autumn to allow the winter frost to break it down, and to use it the following spring. Building began in May; the walls reached full height in one season, and the roof was clad before winter. For example, when Ernest Gimson built a substantial two-storey house of cob in 1911 near Budleigh Salterton, Devon, eight men completed the walls in three months. At this stage cob walls were firm and dry to the touch, but moisture was still present deeper in the fabric.

As they were likely to settle slightly when they dried out completely, a considerable period was allowed to pass before plaster was applied to the surfaces.

A plinth of masonry was built to raise the cob above the reach of rising damp and rain-splash. Traditional buildings did not have guttering; rain was thrown clear of the walls by long overhanging eaves. Houses of cob were rendered with a mixture of finely worked clay and chopped straw, which was renewed at intervals, or with lime plaster, or they were simply lime-washed. For lesser houses this was done only on the front elevation. Many farm buildings and boundary walls were left exposed to the weather except for an overhanging roof of straw. Garden walls of cob are particularly favoured by gardeners: they absorb the sun's heat by day and give it off by night. Fruit trees trained on a cob wall tend to blossom and fruit early.

Well-made cob will last indefinitely if it is protected from the wet, but if it is allowed to become saturated it reverts to a plastic condition and collapses. The commonest causes of structural failure are: (1) damp earth building up around the base; (2) defective roofs and guttering; (3) the accumulation of moisture trapped inside the wall by an impermeable cement render. All earthen materials must be allowed to 'breathe' – to disperse moisture by evaporation. Traditional lime renders repel rain and allow water vapour to disperse. Cement renders, on the other hand, retain any moisture that enters the fabric through cracks or other faults; this water accumulates until the material becomes saturated. Using hard modern cement render on a softer base material always causes problems.

Shuttered earth

Puddled clay and *puddled chalk* are variants of the 'slow process' method of construction. A masonry plinth was built, as for cob. Wooden shuttering was erected on the plinth to a height of about 2 feet (600 mm), known as *boxing*. The earth-straw mixture was prepared in much the same way as for cob and was thrown in and trampled down in shallow layers until the void was filled (puddled chalk can be built without straw, though it is easier to handle with it). The shuttering was left in place until the

A terrace of three cottages of puddled clay on the Lombe Estate at Great Melton, Norfolk, inscribed 'E.L. 1818'. In conversion to one house the doors and windows have been much altered.

material was dry enough to stand unsupported, and then it was moved up to form another course. The advantages of the shuttered method were: (1) material that was too sloppy to stand by itself could be used; (2) the thinner walls made possible by this method required less material; (3) perfectly flat vertical surfaces and sharp arrises (edges) could be formed easily. In other respects shuttered earth has the same characteristics as 'slow process' cob.

Clay lump (also called *clay bat*)

In this method the clay-straw mixture was formed into rectangular blocks about the size of modern concrete blocks. John Curtis of Rougham, Norfolk, in 1842 described how the soft yellow clay, without the addition of chalk or grit, was mixed

Wooden moulds used for making clay lumps, with two lumps (and a house brick for scale). (Photograph by courtesy of Dirk Bouwens)

with water and straw and was trodden by horses.

> As soon as the clay is properly prepared men should make it up into lumps, which is done by putting sufficient clay into a mould of wood, of the following dimensions: 18 inches long, 12 inches wide, and 6 inches deep [450 by 300 by 150 mm] without a bottom. The mould, when well filled by the men putting in the clay with a spade, and pressed with the foot, should be lifted up, and the lump will be left perfect. Wet the mould with a wisp of oat straw to prevent the clay hanging to it, and place the mould about 2 inches [50 mm] from the first lump, and fill as before... This filling of the mould is best done on level grass ground. As soon as the lumps get a little stiff, that is, just enough to admit of handling them, they should be set on one edge, and as they dry be turned; and in doing this place the wet side in the sun.

When firm enough to be lifted, the lumps were stacked to dry in an open pattern. Curtis claimed that in good weather they were ready to be built with after three weeks, but others advised two to three months. In practice it was found that blocks of the size Curtis described were too heavy to lift; more commonly they are 15–18 inches long, 9 inches wide and 6 inches deep (380–450 by 225 by 150 mm). Two men could mould two hundred to four hundred lumps a day from prepared clay.

In much of Essex and East Anglia there is no useful building stone, so the plinth was made of flints, field stones or brickwork, or a combination of these. The dried lumps were laid on the plinth in stretcher bond, using finer clay as mortar. The external walls were 9 inches (225 mm) thick, plus two thicknesses of plaster. For

Clay lumps removed from a nineteenth-century cottage at Broxted, Essex, and a clay-lump wall to the right.

Exposed clay lump in a cottage at High Bridgeham, Norfolk. The partition wall has been newly built; the external wall in the background is original.

internal partitions the same blocks could be laid on edge to make walls 6 inches (150 mm) thick, or thinner blocks could be specially moulded. Many cottages have chimneys of clay lump to roof level, with brickwork above. The walls were finished externally and internally with fine clay-straw mixture – although most of them have now been rendered with lime plaster. Where the render is intact it is difficult to distinguish clay-lump cottages by sight. Many farm buildings of clay lump were left unrendered and were protected from the weather by gas tar or sprayed bitumen.

Using the clay-straw mixture in pre-dried blocks was an important technical innovation because it largely solved the problem of shrinkage. The chalky Boulder Clays of East Anglia are particularly expansive, and aggregates rarely occur naturally in the right proportions. Shrinkage was inevitable, but it occurred

Inside a barn at Ovington, Norfolk, built partly of 'slow process' monolithic clay and partly of clay lump. The builders may have adopted this half-and-half construction to save time, starting monolithic construction while they were waiting for the clay lumps to dry.

while the lumps were stacked to dry, before they were used in the building. Any lumps that distorted or cracked badly were broken up and recycled. The other advantages of this process were: (1) the subsoil available on site could be used without added aggregates; (2) the stacked blocks dried more rapidly than a monolithic wall; (3) when the blocks were dry building could proceed continuously; (4) the thinner walls required less material than traditional cob.

Clay lump had other merits that commended it to improving landlords. In the early nineteenth century they were demolishing roughly built cottages with irregular lines and were building new ones of regular design with straight vertical walls and crisp arrises. Clay lump naturally lent itself to the desired 'neatness' – a word that was used frequently in contemporary descriptions.

Dirk Bouwens has shown that the amount of straw used varied greatly; the lumps that contain the most straw are the strongest and the most resistant to weathering. The same kinds of abuse that can weaken or destroy cob walls affect clay lump in much the same way.

Pisé (or rammed earth)

The *pisé* process was quite different. The subsoil was used dry, without straw or other fibrous material. It was heavily rammed within wooden shuttering so that it consolidated immediately, effectively forming artificial rock. Shallow layers of earth were added and rammed without intervals for drying until the walls reached full height in a day or two. The process required a specially designed wooden frame, strong enough to resist the pressure of ramming, but capable of being dismantled and reassembled as each section was completed. Each length of *pisé*

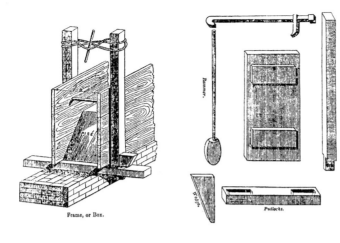

Left: *Illustrations of the equipment used for building in pisé, published by Johnson and Cresey in 1847, but derived from Henry Holland's engravings of 1795. The strongly made shuttering could be dismantled and moved along as each section was completed. The iron tie rod shown to the right would have held the posts more rigidly than the 'Spanish windlass' type of tie shown to the left. The large block formed vertical ends to the pisé for door and window apertures.*

Frame, or Box.

Rammer.

Putlocks.

Right: *A design for a multi-purpose building of pisé, from 'The Cyclopaedia or Universal Dictionary of Arts, Sciences and Literature', edited by A. Rees, 1819, but closely copied from Cointeraux. The elevations show the typical pattern of putlog holes and inclined joints.*

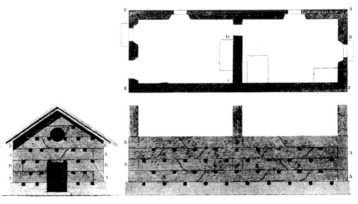

was finished with an inclined end and was overlaid by the next, with the joints staggered. Sometimes the corners were reinforced with rough-sawn boards buried in the material. Apertures were left for doors and windows. Finally, after a period of drying, the putlog holes left by the shuttering were filled and the walls were finished with lime plaster inside and outside.

A *pisé* building can be identified as such only when the plaster is removed. The fabric is harder and denser than cob or shuttered earth, and it does not contain straw or other fibre. It is less affected by saturation. Horizontal lines of putlog holes about 3 feet (900 mm) apart may be visible, although these are now often imperceptible.

In addition to 'pure' earthen walling there are composite structures in which an earth-straw mixture is combined with a light supporting frame or armature of timber and laths. Contemporary records show that these *mud and stud* buildings have been built in many parts of England, but most of those that survive are in Lincolnshire. In north-east Scotland there are many examples of *daubed palisade* buildings. These and turf walling are outside the scope of this book, but see works by Cousins and Walker in the 'Further reading' section.

The history of earthen walling

It has been estimated that one-third of the world's population lives in mud houses. The simplest dwellings are made by weaving pliant rods together to form a basket-like structure, and daubing it with mud mixed with any natural fibre. A similar material, *wattle and daub*, was used in Britain for many centuries (and still gives good service), but here it forms the panels in a substantial timber frame. In these buildings the wooden components provide much of the structural strength, but in cob, shuttered earth and *pisé* the material has its own strength, requiring timber only to bridge over door and window apertures and for roofs and floors.

Unfired bricks of mud and straw six thousand years old have been excavated at Hassuna in Iraq; others have been found in many ancient cultures. In the first century BC Vitruvius described the use of unfired bricks of shallow rectangular shape containing straw. In the first century AD Pliny described earthen walls built within formwork in Spain and north Africa, probably similar to the walls of rammed earth that can be seen there today.

A 1797 engraving by J. T. Smith of a cottage in Enfield, Middlesex, with garden walls of mud evidently built up in layers – one of the few depictions of this period in which the method may be identified.

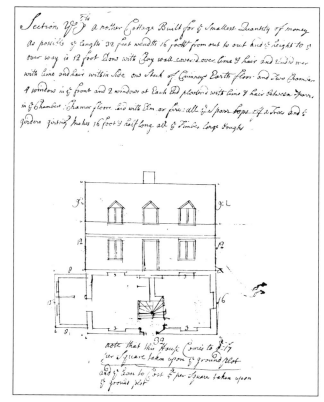

Section y[e] 5th a nother Cottage Built for [ye] Smallest Quantity of money as possible [ye] Length 32 feet weadth 16 foott from out to out and [ye] height to [ye] over way is 12 foot Done with Clay wall cover'd over Lime [&] hair and Ended over with Lime and hair within Side on Stack of Guinneys Earth floor and Two Chamber [&] window in [ye] front and 2 windows at Each End plastord with Lime [&] hair Between [ye]arr, in [ye] Chambers Chamor floore Laid with Elm or fire: all [ye] spaar tops of a tree and [ye] girdors girsing Inches 16 foot [&] haif long all [ye] Timbes Large toughs

note that this House Comis to [£]-17 [per] square taken upon [ye] ground [plot] and [ye] Lean to [£] oot [&] [per] square taken upon [ye] ground [plot]

The design and specification of a 'Cottage built for the Smallest Quantity of money as possible' by James Deane of Colchester: 'Done with Clay wall cover'd over [with] lime & hair and rended [rendered] over with lime and hair within Side'. The type of clay construction was not specified but would have been cob or puddled clay. The illustration is undated, but Deane lived 1699–1765. This is the cheaper of two designs. Cottages of this quality were not provided for farm labourers in the lifetime of James Deane but were more likely to be built for minor freeholders. (By courtesy of Essex Record Office)

In dry climates archaeological evidence of earthen walls may survive, but in the wetter conditions of Britain they tend to revert to mud soon after they are abandoned. At *Verulamium*, St Albans, Hertfordshire, S. S. Frere has excavated Roman walls of 'clean yellow clay' formed between boards on a stone foundation, with putlog holes at intervals of 8 feet (2.44 metres). Low walls of clay packed between shuttering of wattle, dating from the Viking period, have been excavated at York, Norwich, London and elsewhere.

The place name Mudwall is recorded in London from 1395 and in Essex from 1497. The Welsh name Pontypridd means 'the bridge by the earthen house'. In 1540 John Leland described the fortifications of Henry VIII's naval base at Portsmouth as 'a mudde wall armid with timbre'; the wall supported artillery. The great strength of mud fortifications must have been in John Locke's mind in 1640 when he wrote 'Earthly minds, like Mud-walls, resist the strongest batteries'.

Cob and shuttered earth

Historic records of all periods include brief references to buildings and boundary walls of mud and clay, but they do not describe how they were built. Before the late eighteenth century writers regarded the dwellings of the common people as beneath their notice. From 1775 humanitarian reformers began to express their concern about the squalid conditions in which most farmworkers lived; they tried to persuade rural landlords that it was in their interest to build improved cottages for their tenants. The movement had little practical effect until the 1790s, and then only in 'closed parishes' where one landlord owned all the land. In 'open parishes', where ownership was more dispersed, there was resistance from other ratepayers; they feared that providing better cottages would attract more people into the parish and so increase the poor rate. The Poor Law Amendment Act of 1834 ended this objection. Cottages sprang up everywhere. In 1843 Copinger Hill wrote: 'Cottages are too much in the hands of speculators, who exact an exorbitant rent for very inferior accommodation.' He and other housing reformers showed that it was possible to provide well-built cottages with two ground-floor rooms and two bedrooms above at rents that farmworkers could pay. In this period architects and progressive land agents produced a substantial literature on cottage building, which now provides us with contemporary descriptions of all the earth-building processes then in use.

From 1784 a tax on bricks, which added some 15 per cent to their cost, supplied an extra incentive for landlords and builders to consider the merits of building with unfired earth. The material cost only the wages for digging, and the straw. The subsoil was extracted near the building site, so there was no expenditure on carting (a pond in a cottage garden indicates where the subsoil came from). No fuel was consumed. In the model cottages described by Copinger Hill clay walls cost £17; stone walls cost £39, plus the cost of transport from the quarry. Brick was even more expensive; he recommended it only for chimneys and ovens. Writers in Devon calculated that the cost of a cob wall, including the stone plinth, was only 60 per cent of the cost of an equivalent wall of stone.

Clay lump (or *clay bat*)

This method of building had long been used in drier climates elsewhere in the world, but in Britain it was a late development.

Nest-boxes made of clay bats in a timber-framed dovecote at Steeple Bumpstead, Essex.

Reputable authors writing before 1987 (including C. F. Innocent, Clough Williams-Ellis, Maurice Barley and Alec Clifton-Taylor) claimed that in Norfolk and Suffolk it was a traditional way of building, and that there were farmhouses three hundred years old built of clay lump. This assertion has been shown to be a fallacy; no standing buildings of clay lump earlier than the nineteenth century have been identified.

Late in the eighteenth century thin *bats* of chalky clay mixed with straw were used to form the nest-boxes of dovecotes in Cambridgeshire and Essex, where the main structure was of other materials. In June 1791 an ingenious bricklayer named Joseph Austin, who had made clay bats for dovecotes, began to build himself a cottage of the same material at Great Shelford, 4 miles (6 km) south of Cambridge; it became the first building in England *structurally composed* of clay bats. The Reverend James Plumptree admired Austin's cottage and questioned him about it; he published an account of it in 1801. The story of Joseph Austin's initiative attracted the attention of the Poet Laureate, Robert Southey, who told it again to a much wider readership in 1816. In Austin's cottage the bats were only 3 inches (76 mm) thick, like the shallow slabs used to form the nest-boxes of dovecotes. By 1821 there were many cottages, small ancillary buildings and garden walls of clay bats in that part of Cambridgeshire. Probably many of them were built by Joseph Austin and his large family of sons and nephews, who were all bricklayers.

In 1821 John Denson, a market gardener, published an account of the method in a Cambridge newspaper, and in 1823 he built himself a cottage of the same material at Waterbeach. The blocks he described were 6 inches (150 mm) deep; his description is the first known use of the term 'clay lumps'. It was quoted by J. C. Loudon in his *Encyclopaedia of Cottage, Farm and Villa Architecture*, described there as a Cambridgeshire technique. The *Encyclopaedia* was revised and reissued many times, and was immensely influential. John Curtis's account of making clay lumps in Norfolk first appeared in the edition of 1847.

In the period 1820–40 whole farmyards in Norfolk were rebuilt in clay lump. This one is at Southburgh, Norfolk The surfaces were protected from the weather by gas tar, much of which has flaked away.

A pair of estate cottages of clay lump (now converted into one house) at Woodrising, Norfolk, built by Ignatius Wayland in 1827.

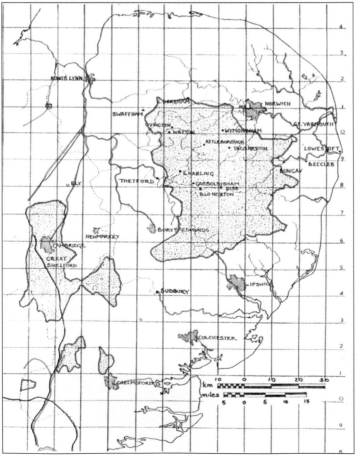

The main areas of East Anglia and Essex where buildings of clay lump are found, outlined in red. One area is centred on Great Shelford, 4 miles (6 km) south of Cambridge, where the method was initiated by Joseph Austin from 1791 and publicised locally by John Denson. The larger area corresponds with the watershed zone of south Norfolk and north Suffolk. Navigable waterways are marked in blue. County boundaries are shown dotted. (By courtesy of Dirk Bouwens)

In the period 1820–40 an agricultural revolution was in progress in Norfolk and Suffolk. The heavy clay lands that formerly had been used as pasture were being deep-drained and converted to arable. Whole farmsteads were rebuilt, and many new cottages were required. Where coastal or river transport was available the agricultural improvers built with established materials, but in the watershed zone between the east-flowing and west-flowing rivers, where only expensive transport by horse and wagon was available, they were glad to adopt the new clay-lump process. That is why there are more clay-lump buildings in that area of Norfolk and Suffolk than anywhere else. A similar innovation was reported in Perthshire in 1792, but there it was not adopted on a comparable scale because local agricultural developments were at a different stage.

Pisé (or rammed earth)

Pisé was a traditional form of construction in the Rhône valley of France, in parts of Spain and in north-west Africa, where the soils and climate are particularly suitable; it is still practised in Morocco. In 1772 George-Claude Goiffon described the method in *L'Art du maçon piseur*. From 1791 François Cointeraux took it up with enthusiasm; he produced adaptable designs and a series of manuals, which were translated into other languages. In 1795 Francis Russell, fifth Duke of Bedford, and his architect Henry Holland introduced the process at Woburn Park, Bedfordshire, and built estate cottages of *pisé* in nearby villages. Holland published an English translation of Cointeraux's instructions, recommending *pisé* to the newly formed Board of Agriculture as

A pair of pisé cottages at Ridgmont, Bedfordshire, built in 1798 – one of the few surviving pisé buildings erected for the fifth Duke of Bedford. At the far end the pisé has been rebuilt in brickwork.

19

highly suitable for farmworkers' cottages. Because the process was introduced at this high social level it was described in favourable terms by sycophantic imitators who had no personal experience of it. In fact it was not a great success at Woburn, or in many of the places where it was tried; most of the *pisé* buildings at or near Woburn have been demolished. *Pisé* was never generally adopted in Britain; it is not difficult to see why: (1) it required special formwork of sophisticated design; (2) the ramming required much arduous labour, and still the structure could fail if the work was not closely supervised; (3) under aristocratic influence it was adopted in places where the soil was not ideally suitable. Instructions for building with *pisé* continued to be copied from book to book until late in the nineteenth century by authors who had not built with it. Eventually they were reprinted in handbooks intended for emigrants to Canada, Australia and New Zealand. However, in England the influence of the fifth Duke declined after his death in 1802. The sixth Duke abandoned *pisé* and used brickwork for all new buildings.

From the mid nineteenth century several factors combined to cause building with earth to lose favour, although it continued to be practised on a reduced scale. In 1850 the Brick Tax was abolished. During the 1860s and 1870s the brick industry became increasingly mechanised. The main railway network had been completed, enabling mass-produced bricks to be transported economically from distant sources. It was an industrial age; standardised industrial products were preferred to the vernacular equivalents. From 1875 arable farming fell into deep depression owing to competition with cheap grain from North America. Within a few years livestock-farming areas were almost equally affected by cheap imports of refrigerated meat. Farmworkers left the land to seek work in the towns, or to emigrate; the building of farm cottages ceased. By the time agriculture had recovered sufficiently to require more cottages brick had become the generally accepted building material.

Even in rural Devon, where the cob tradition was most firmly established, by the second half of the nineteenth century most farmhouses and farm buildings were built of stone rubble with brick dressings, made possible by improved supplies of lime and bricks brought by rail. Cob was cheaper; its use continued, but mainly for the less important farm buildings.

Farnham, Dorset – a village street largely of cob. The plinths are of flint and brickwork.

The regional pattern

Cob

Cob buildings are more likely to be found on the floors of wide valleys than on their steep sides. The reason is that the clay soils of which they are composed were formed from the sedimentary material washed down the slopes to settle at the bottom. Cob buildings are found also on fairly flat land, made from the deep beds of clay and chalk that were laid down in remote geological eras.

The largest concentration of cob buildings extends across the south-west of England from Cornwall to Hampshire. Devon has most of all, estimated in tens of thousands. There are standing buildings of cob from the fourteenth and fifteenth centuries, and from all later periods. Fashionable villas for the gentry, including three-storeyed town houses, continued to be built of cob until the middle of the nineteenth century; often this is not recognised until the plaster is removed. The material varies greatly in colour, from deep red and red-brown on the Permian Sandstones to buff or grey on the Culm Measures. The skill of the local practitioners must command our respect, for the geology of Devon is highly varied; cob construction has been used successfully with widely different soils.

In Cornwall cob buildings and garden walls are found in many lowland areas, but particularly the Lizard peninsula and the eastern part of the county. It is common to encounter houses in which the ground storey is built of stone and the upper storey of cob. In Somerset cob buildings exist in numerous

Right: Marker's Cottage, Broadclyst, Devon, a fifteenth-century house belonging to the National Trust. It is open to the public.

Cob cottages at Broadclyst, Devon.

Left: *A fifteenth-century cob house with jointed crucks in Sidbury, Devon, and an eighteenth-century house beyond.*

Above: *Inside a cob cottage at Down St Mary, Devon; note the deep window reveal, the rounded arris and the contemporary window.*

Left: *An early-nineteenth-century villa in Sidmouth, Devon, where there are many town houses of cob.*

A whole farmyard of exposed cob near Brampford Speke, Devon. The raises are clearly visible to the left.

places, roughly corresponding with the Keuper Marls, but they have not survived in very large numbers. Many have been destroyed by floods.

As one proceeds eastwards across Wiltshire and Dorset to Hampshire the clay soils give way to chalk. After Devon, Dorset has the next highest number of cob buildings, although many are not easily recognised as such by the casual visitor. The material is creamy white; here it is called *mud* or *chalk mud*. Garden walls of

Right: *Slate-hung cottages of cob at Bray Shop, Cornwall.*

Left: *An early-nineteenth-century house of cob at North Petherwin, Cornwall, with the original hipped roof of Cornish slate. The south-west wall, which receives most of the driving rain, is protected by hung slates.*

A house of cob at Stratton, Cornwall. The nearer part is the older.

A barn of cob at Bilbrook, Somerset.

A cob barn at Elworthy, Somerset, that was originally thatched. At the far end part of it has been rebuilt with concrete blocks.

A house of exposed cob at Week St Mary, Cornwall, on a foundation wall of stone rubble. Minor erosion has left sharp stones projecting from the surface, but it seldom proceeds any further. The lintels are of slate.

A house of cob at Roadwater, Somerset.

mud occur wherever there are chalky soils; they are often the most visible indication that the adjacent houses may be of mud too. Originally they were thatched, but many now have copings of tiles. The houses and cottages of chalk mud are most easily identified by their high plinths of flint, stone or brickwork, visibly different in texture from the walls above.

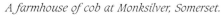

A farmhouse of cob at Monksilver, Somerset.

Thomas Hardy's cottage at Higher Bockhampton, Dorset. This view from the back shows that the cottage is built mainly of cob. It is owned by the National Trust and is open to the public.

Cottages of cob at Tolpuddle, Dorset – the village the Tolpuddle Martyrs came from.

A cob cottage at Winterborne Whitechurch, Dorset, being re-thatched. The high plinth of brick and flint is visible.

Above: *A village street largely of cob, Bere Regis, Dorset.*

Right: *The early-nineteenth-century Gothic lodge and linked wall at Maddington Manor, Wiltshire.*

A barn of chalk mud beside the river Ebble at Coombe Bissett, Wiltshire.

27

The village of Milton Abbas, Dorset, was rebuilt on a new site about 1790 as part of a major landscaping scheme to improve the view from the house of the squire, Joseph Damer. The architect of the new model village is believed to have been Sir William Chambers. The mud cottages were built as attached pairs, now combined, and originally were roofed with heather thatch.

Above: A thatched cob wall at Dorchester-on-Thames, Oxfordshire. The sandy colour shows that this is not witchert though it is near the witchert area. The plinth of stone rubble is clearly visible.

Right: A barn and farmyard wall of chalk mud at Coombe Bissett, Wiltshire.

A particular form of cob walling known as *witchert* (the name is variously spelt, but derives from 'white earth') occurs in Buckinghamshire and Oxfordshire, in a belt extending from south-west of Aylesbury through Thame to Dorchester-on-Thames. The high content of decomposed limestone in the clay subsoil makes it ideally suitable for witchert building. The courses (the local word is *berries*) may stand 3 feet (900 mm) high or

A witchert cottage being thatched at Haddenham, Buckinghamshire.

A witchert cottage at Haddenham, Buckinghamshire. The Victorian house in the background is also of witchert.

Right: *Haddenham Baptist Church, Buckinghamshire, built of witchert in 1822 to a strictly formal design with crisp outlines. The height of the walls indicates the extraordinary stability of this local form of cob.*

Garden walls of witchert at Haddenham, Buckinghamshire, only 9 inches (230 mm) thick. Without capping or maintenance the wall to the right is crumbling away, but the capped and rendered wall to the left is in perfect order.

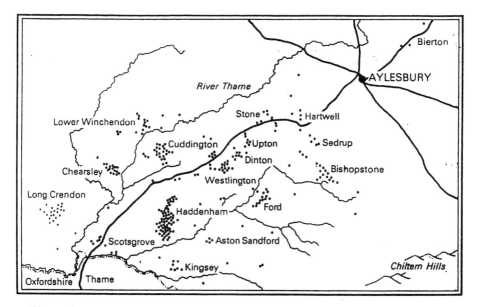

Buildings of witchert in Buckinghamshire. (By courtesy of Martin Andrew and 'Country Life' magazine)

more while wet without slumping. The material sets so rapidly that work could proceed continuously. Witchert can stand to a height of 20 feet (6 metres), as may be seen in the two Nonconformist churches of Haddenham. Garden walls may be only 9 inches (230 mm) thick.

There is another concentration of 'slow process' buildings in the East Midlands – in Leicestershire, Northamptonshire, Rutland, south-east Nottinghamshire and eastern Warwickshire. The material is yellow-brown in colour, formed from the Liassic subsoil, and is

A mud boundary wall at Saddington, Leicestershire. Originally it would have been thatched. The base has been repaired with brickwork.

31

known locally as *mud*. It is built on high foundation walls of stone rubble of the same colour. The mud walls of houses are often between 2 feet and 2 feet 6 inches (600–750 mm) thick at the base, decreasing to 1 foot 6 inches (450 mm) at the top. They rarely stand more than 8 or 9 feet (2.40–3 metres) above the plinth. Farmhouses and cottages were rendered with lime plaster; there are numerous examples in Billesdon, Great Dalby, Harby and Saddington. Farm buildings and boundary walls were left unrendered; the roofs and copings were of thatch originally, but now most of them are of corrugated iron, tiles or slates. The short overhang of modern roofs has exposed the vertical surfaces to rainwater, causing progressive erosion. In this area houses of the

*This farmhouse
at Great Creaton,
Northampton-
shire, has a gable
wall of stone and
side walls of
mud.*

Early-nineteenth-century mud cottages at Dunchurch, Warwickshire. Note the deep reveals of the original windows to the right.

Left: *A farmhouse at Nether Broughton, Leicestershire. Originally built of mud to a height of one and a half storeys, later it was raised to two full storeys with brickwork.*

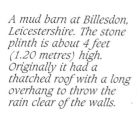

A mud barn at Billesdon, Leicestershire. The stone plinth is about 4 feet (1.20 metres) high. Originally it had a thatched roof with a long overhang to throw the rain clear of the walls.

The Old Post Office at Great Dalby, Leicestershire. Buttresses often reveal that the construction is of mud, as here.

gentry were always of stone; the mud buildings never commanded the same respect.

On the Solway Plain of Cumbria there is another group of clay farmhouses, farm buildings and cottages known locally as *clay dabbins*. They were described in 1962 in an innovative study by R. W. Brunskill and since then have been studied by J. R. Harrison, Nina Jennings, Peter Messenger and others. Here a different method was employed, which Brunskill has called the 'quick process'. Contemporary accounts record that a whole community would assemble to build the walls of a house for a newly married couple, completing them in one day. The mud was laid in shallow courses about 3 inches (76 mm) deep, each

A clay dabbin at Longburgh, Cumbria. Originally it was of one storey throughout. The central part with small square windows remains the least altered, still open to the roof, with a large fire-hood of clay-daubed wicker. Note the deep window reveals. (Photograph by courtesy of J. R. Harrison)

A clay dabbin at Fingland, Cumbria. Originally this was built as a single-storey house of two rooms with a down-house to the right (which has been extended). The only original window aperture is the small fire-window. (Photograph by courtesy of J. R. Harrison)

covered by a layer of straw. Much of the weight of the thatched roof was taken by purlins and a ridge supported on crucks; effectively the rafters were hung from the ridge, their feet resting freely on the long walls. The earliest clay dabbins that survive date from the seventeenth century; most are of the eighteenth and early nineteenth centuries. Other buildings constructed by the more familiar 'slow process' exist in this area too.

In Wales mud was used extensively for cottages and farm buildings in the nineteenth century, and for some farmhouses earlier; it is correctly called *clom* in the west and *mwd* in the north. The material varies from yellow clay to grey mud containing flakes of stone and often was mixed

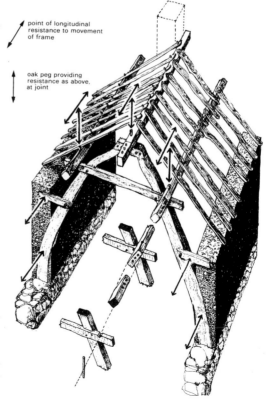

point of longitudinal resistance to movement of frame

oak peg providing resistance as above, at joint

Three-dimensional diagram of a typical clay dabbin farmhouse of the Solway Plain, showing how most of the weight of the thatched roof is carried by crucks supporting a ridge-piece and purlins, and how this construction resists longitudinal stresses. (By courtesy of J. R. Harrison)

35

A derelict nineteenth-century cottage and cow-house at Esgair, Carmarthenshire. The foundation wall and quoins are of stone, the rest is of clom. The walls are 2 feet (600 mm) thick, with a chimney of clom up to roof level. The corrugated iron roof was laid over the thatch to avoid the cost of re-thatching.

Right: A derelict cottage at Blaenporth, Ceredigion, with a corrugated iron roof over the original thatch. The gable chimney is of clom up to roof level (erosion has caused it to break through in places).

A clom farmhouse at Llanfihangel Ystrad, Ceredigion. Unlike later buildings, it is built to a 'running level' parallel with the ground.

An empty cottage of clom at Temple Bar, Ceredigion. The front has been cement-rendered; the clom fabric is visible to the right, much eroded by weather.

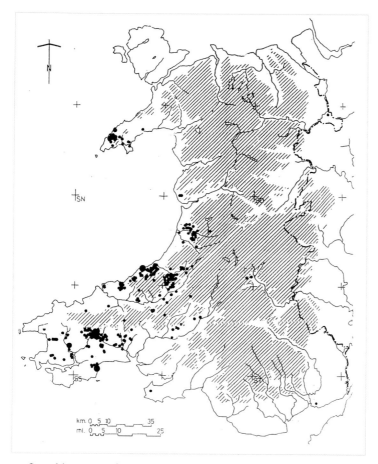

Confirmed locations of clom-walled buildings in Wales, prepared by Gerallt D. Nash, Museum of Welsh Life, St Fagans.

with *Juncus* marsh grass rather than straw. The 'quick process' was used in Wales also. Often *clom* and stone walling are combined in the same building. Single-storey cottages may have the front wall (containing a door and two windows) mainly of stone, with the other three walls of *clom*. Gable-end chimneys are of *clom* up to the roof, with stone or brick above. Two-storey farm buildings can be of stone to first-floor level, with the upper part of *clom*. The distribution of surviving examples is now wholly western. There are survivals in many parts of the south-west, with concentrations in west Carmarthen and the Aeron valley, and a smaller number in the Lleyn peninsula of Gwynedd. Most mud cottages are abandoned now, but some are occupied and well maintained. One from Nant Walter has been dismantled and reconstructed at the Museum of Welsh Life at St Fagans.

In Scotland Alexander Fenton and Bruce Walker have shown that there is a long tradition of building with clay in all the eastern

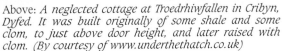

Above: *A neglected cottage at Troedrhiwfallen in Cribyn, Dyfed. It was built originally of some shale and some clom, to just above door height, and later raised with clom. (By courtesy of www.underthethatch.co.uk)*

Right: *The interior of a restored clom cottage at Ffynnon Oer, Ceredigion. Note the vernacular quality of the roof framing and rafters. A wood-burning stove has been placed in the former fireplace, under the original smoke hood of wicker and clom. (By courtesy of www.underthethatch.co.uk)*

A house of clom from Nant Walter, dismantled and rebuilt at the Museum of Welsh Life, St Fagans. (Photograph by courtesy of the National Museums and Galleries of Wales)

This farm building at Flatfield, Perthshire, is of cob, built in 1784. The 'needles' of the tie-beams grip the relatively soft walls to resist the outward stress of the roof. It has been roughly rendered with modern cement.

Right: *This building at Errol, Perthshire, is of cob up to eaves level, with a gable of brickwork. The front elevation has been 'ashlared' – inscribed with straight lines in the render to imitate ashlar stonework.*

counties from Dornoch in Sutherland to Berwick-upon-Tweed. The cob process was usually called *clay dab*; the fibrous material incorporated included heather, bracken, broom and rushes. In Dumfries and Galloway buildings similar to those of Cumbria were formerly common, but few have survived.

Shuttered earth

Buildings and boundary walls of shuttered earth are found mainly on landed estates because the shuttering was not economical unless used on a substantial scale. In Devon this method was used from 1820. It is common in Norfolk and Suffolk and has been found in north Essex; most buildings of shuttered earth date from the early nineteenth century. Puddled chalk is common in Dorset, Wiltshire and Hampshire, where its use continued until 1914. In north-eastern Scotland there were variant techniques such as *clay and bool*, in which stones of similar size were laid in clay-straw mixture in regular courses against the inside of shuttering packed with puddled clay. The finished building presents an appearance of coursed stone or herringbone patterns. In the later nineteenth century a technique was developed in Perthshire in which a thin casing of brickwork or stone was used to form the outer skin for puddled clay construction and was left permanently in place. There are houses in the main street of Errol that have front elevations of brick – the

An early-nineteenth-century cottage at Kettlebaston, Suffolk – one of several there of identical design. Three walls are of puddled clay 13 inches (330 mm) thick. The near gable end is of puddled clay only up to eaves level, and of light timber framing above. The far gable end comprised a brick chimney, with the space to each side closed with timber framing. Originally there was only one upstairs room, at the near end – although most of these cottages have been altered and extended since. This was a typical improved farmworker's dwelling of the period.

Right: *A boundary wall of puddled chalk near Winterslow, Wiltshire. No straw is apparent in the fabric.*

Below: *This building in Errol, Perthshire, has a street elevation of brick and a side elevation of stone, but the walls are mainly of puddled clay. The brick skin is in stretcher bond, only 4¹/₂ inches (114 mm) thick.*

most prized material at the time – and side and rear elevations of stone rubble, but in which the fabric is mainly of puddled clay.

Clay lump and clay bat

Early-nineteenth-century cottages of *clay bats* – the local name – are common in south Cambridgeshire and north-west Essex, but they are difficult to recognise because the material is now concealed by plaster outside and inside. They are more likely to be found on enclosed waste and the outskirts of villages than in the centres, because the best sites were already occupied before the method was developed. The earliest ones were built with shallow bats 3–4 inches (75–100 mm) deep. Scattered cottages, terraces and outhouses of clay lump occur in other parts of

Above left: Built originally to house steam traction engines at East Harling, Norfolk, with walls 26 feet (8 metres) high, this may be the largest building ever constructed of clay lump in Britain. It has been demolished for redevelopment.

Above: Clay lump with clay mortar. The straw incorporated in the lumps is visible. The surface has been damaged by the attachment of a cement render.

Left: This illustration shows how the brick facing was tied to a wall of clay lump. Strips of hoop iron were nailed to the clay wall and built into the courses of brickwork. Black Car, Norfolk.

Essex, Hertfordshire and Bedfordshire, but seldom other kinds of buildings. Landowners and builders read of the method in Loudon's *Encyclopaedia* and tried it out on a small scale. The economies that resulted were rarely so impressive as to persuade them to build many more.

The largest concentration of clay-lump buildings is in south Norfolk and north Suffolk. Here clay lump was used for buildings of all kinds – a corn exchange, a hotel, schools, chapels, maltings, mills and other industrial buildings, as well as numerous farmhouses, farm buildings and cottages. Some of the later buildings were faced with brick, particularly in the towns; there are numerous examples in Attleborough.

These are the main concentrations of vernacular earthen buildings in Britain today, but historical records and occasional survivals show that earth has been used in many other places, even where good building stone was easily available.

A clay-lump house faced with brickwork at Attleborough, Norfolk.

The White House, King's Somborne, Hampshire, built of chalk pisé in the early nineteenth century.

A rustic lodge at Marden Ash, near Chipping Ongar, Essex. Dirk Bouwens identified the fabric as pisé after a disastrous thatch fire; he found that it was 'made of gravel containing a lot of iron oxide'. It is shown here after restoration. No other buildings of pisé have been found in the district. (Photograph by courtesy of Dirk Bouwens)

Pisé (or rammed earth)

The *pisé* process was less successful in Britain than the architectural literature may suggest. Gordon Pearson has shown that gentry houses of *pisé* were built in the chalk belt of Hampshire in the early part of the nineteenth century, probably because the local chalky soil was easily compacted. In Winchester he relates it to railway construction, which produced large amounts of surplus chalk. Elsewhere in England *pisé* buildings are extremely rare. They are always non-vernacular, built to the designs of the gentry, and always prove to date from the early years of the nineteenth century. In Britain *pisé* was a short-lived fashion.

Council houses of clay lump at East Harling, Norfolk, built by George Skipper in the late 1920s.

Survivals and revival

In 1904 Sir Walter Gilbey built superior two-storey cottages of clay lump on his estate at Elsenham, Essex, clad with weatherboarding. In 1911, when Ernest Gimson wanted to build a house of cob near Budleigh Salterton, Devon, he found one man who had worked with cob thirty years earlier. During the First World War J. St Loe Strachey experimented with *pisé* at Newlands Corner, Surrey, where the subsoil is chalk. He reported that a platoon of soldiers who had not worked with *pisé* before completed the walls of a building 20 feet square by 10 feet high (6 metres by 3 metres) in ten hours. In 1919 Clough Williams-Ellis published a book describing all the earth-building methods, proposing that earth was the answer to a pressing contemporary problem, a massive shortage of building materials. It attracted much interest, and the Government's Department of Scientific and Industrial Research built some experimental cottages at Amesbury, Wiltshire. Colonel Frank Bernard of Winchendon, Buckinghamshire, had some witchert cottages built there in the

One of the weatherboarded clay-lump cottages built by Sir Walter Gilbey in 1904 on his estate at Elsenham and Molehill Green, Essex. Originally they were of identical design, but many of them have since been altered. The occupant of this cottage told the author that it was the most comfortable house she had ever lived in because it was always warm in winter and cool in summer.

Above: *The bus shelter at Down St Mary, Devon, built by Alfred Howard in 1978, which initiated the revival of cob building in Devon.*

Left: *Alfred Howard, master builder, demonstrating how to make up small quantities of cob for repairs. He has contributed a sound knowledge of traditional practice to the revival of cob building in Devon.*

late 1920s. At the same period the architect George Skipper was building council houses of clay lump at East Harling, Norfolk. The main building industry continued to ignore earth as a building material, no doubt because it yielded little profit.

After the Second World War John and Elizabeth Eastwick-Field revised and re-published Williams-Ellis's book, but they were no more successful in influencing the building industry. In Devon the need to keep the numerous cob buildings in repair had some limited effect in keeping the traditional skills alive. In 1978 the master builder Alfred Howard demonstrated that cob was still a viable material for new buildings by constructing a bus shelter at Down St Mary, Devon; since then he has played a major part in the revival of cob building. The technologies of cob building have been studied primarily to secure appropriate repairs to the numerous listed buildings. Advisory papers have been published by the Devon Historic Buildings Trust and the Devon Earth Building Association (DEBA); other studies and training courses are in progress at the Centre for Earthen Architecture of Plymouth University. DEBA has held many informative meetings, and a new generation of cob builders has emerged in Devon.

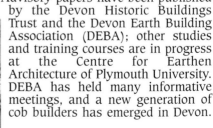

Cob made into blocks by Alfred Howard, used mainly for repairs. The nearest block is about the size of a typical East Anglian clay lump.

Summer-house of cob at Marker's Cottage, Broadclyst, Devon, built for the National Trust to celebrate the millennium year 2000. Designed by Jill Smallcombe, executed by Chris Brookman.

Below: *Modern garden wall of cob by Mathew Robinson at St Martin, near Helston, Cornwall, illustrating the sculptural possibilities of the material. (Photograph by courtesy of Mathew Robinson)*

Since 1984 EARTHA, the East Anglian equivalent of DEBA, has explored the techniques of repairing clay buildings in East Anglia, and has held public demonstrations. In the East Midlands a local interest group, the East Midlands Earth Structures Society (EMESS), is active.

Some new buildings of cob have been built in Cornwall, Devon and elsewhere. Although some of the manual work has been mechanised, cob is no longer a cheap material; it appeals mainly to enthusiasts and to those who want a house of individual character. Increasingly it is accepted by local authorities and building inspectors, particularly as the

A house of pisé being built at Taurikura, Whaukerei Heads, New Zealand, in 1986. Modern shuttering does not leave the putlog holes that are characteristic of pisé in England. (Photograph by courtesy of Magdalen McCann)

A three-storey house of cob at Ottery St Mary, Devon, built by Kevin McCabe in 2002.

Left: *A new ancillary building of cob being built at Ottery St Mary, Devon, in 2003, by Kevin McCabe. The first two raises, or courses, of the building.*

Below: *Kevin McCabe's men at work on the building. The material is forked on to the wall, where they press and hammer it into position with their boots. Later the vertical surfaces will be trimmed down with a sharp spade.*

initial construction consumes so much less energy than industrial products. Cob builders can at last claim that they are working along nationally approved guidelines.

Outside Britain there has been a substantial revival of earthen building, stimulated by the French organisation CRATerre. There are parts of the world in which local conditions – under-employment, cheap labour or remoteness from the sources of industrial products – recall the economic conditions of early-nineteenth-century Britain. This book is primarily about Britain, but an example of new *pisé* building in New Zealand is illustrated on page 45.

Further reading

Most of the reliable information on this subject was written either before 1850, when building with earth was still widely practised, or after 1980. In the interim the craft traditions were effectively lost; authors who wrote about the forgotten technologies were sometimes misled by romantic misconceptions or inaccurate observation. Their contributions to the literature should be read with this reservation in mind. To this generalisation R. W. Brunskill's 1962 study of the clay dabbins of Cumberland is a notable exception.

Andrew, Martin. 'Walls with Hats On: Witchert Buildings of Buckinghamshire', *Country Life*, 2nd October 1986.

Beacham, Peter (editor). *Devon Building: An Introduction to Local Traditions*. Devon Books/Halsgrove Publishing, 2000.

Bouwens, Dirk. 'Clay Lump in South Norfolk: Observations and Recollections', *Vernacular Architecture*, 19 (1988).

Brunskill, R. W. 'The Clay Houses of Cumberland', *Transactions of the Ancient Monuments Society*, 10 (1962).

Cousins, Rodney. *Lincolnshire Building in the Mud and Stud Tradition*. Heritage Lincolnshire, Sleaford, Lincolnshire, 2000.

Devon Historic Buildings Trust and Devon Earth Building Association. Papers on conserving cob from 1992 onwards.

Harrison, J. R. 'The Mud Wall in England at the Close of the Vernacular Era', *Transactions of the Ancient Monuments Society*, 28 (1984).

Harrison, J. R. 'Some Clay Dabbins in Cumberland: Their Construction and Form', *Transactions of the Ancient Monuments Society*, 33 (1989) and 35 (1991).

Harrison, J. R. *Earth: The Conservation and Repair of Bowhill, Exeter – Working with Cob*. James & James for English Heritage, 2000.

Hill, Copinger. 'On the Construction of Cottages', *Journal of the Royal Agricultural Society*, 4 (1843).

Holland, Henry. 'On Cottages', *Appendix to Communications to the Board of Agriculture*, 1 (1797).

Houben, H., and Guillaud, H. *Earth Construction: A Comprehensive Guide*. CRATerre, Grenoble, 1994.

Hurd, John, and Gourlay, Ben (editors). *Terra Britannica: A Celebration of Earthen Structures in Great Britain*. James & James for English Heritage and ICOMOS, 2000.

Jennings, Nina. 'The Building of the Clay Dabbins of the Solway Plain: Materials and Man-Hours', *Vernacular Architecture*, 33 (2002).

Johnson, C. W., and Cresey, E. *On the Cottages of Agricultural Labourers*. London, 1847.

McCann, John. 'Warm in Winter, Cool in Summer: Mud Buildings of the East Midlands', *Country Life*, 11th November 1982.

McCann, John. 'Is Clay Lump a Traditional Building Material?', *Vernacular Architecture*, 18 (1987).

McCann, John. 'The First Cottage of Clay Bats?', *Proceedings of the Cambridge Antiquarian Society*, 76 (1987).

McCann, John. 'The Origin of Clay Lump in England', *Vernacular Architecture*, 28 (1997).

Minke, Gernot. *Earth Construction Handbook*. Wit Press, 2000.

Norton, J. *Building with Earth: A Handbook*. IT Publications, 1986.

Pearson, Gordon. *The Conservation of Clay and Chalk Buildings*. Donhead, 1992.

Schofield, J., and Smallcombe, J. *Cob Building: A Practical Guide*. Black Dog Press, Crediton, 2004.

Walker, Bruce *et al*. *Earth Structures and Conservation in Scotland*. Historic Scotland, 1996.

Warren, John. *Conservation of Earth Structures*. Butterworth Heinemann, 1999.

Wiliam, E. *Home-Made Homes: Dwellings of the Rural Poor in Wales*. National Museums and Galleries of Wales, 1988.

Williams-Ellis, Clough. *Cottage Building in Cob, Pisé, Chalk and Clay*. Country Life, 1919.

Other sources of information

Specialist advice on the conservation and repair of earthen buildings in Britain can be obtained from:

The Society for the Protection of Ancient Buildings, 37 Spital Square, London E1 6DY.
English Heritage, 23 Savile Row, London W1X 1AB.
Cadw (Welsh Historic Monuments), Brunel House, 2 Fitzalan Road, Cardiff CF2 1UY.
Historic Scotland, 20 Brandon Street, Edinburgh EH3 5RA.

County and District Councils have Conservation Officers who can advise or put the enquirer in touch with DEBA, EARTHA or EMESS.

Index